Begin the Search

FINDING YOUR MARRIAGE

ERIC HITCHENS

TATE PUBLISHING
AND ENTERPRISES, LLC

Published by Tate Publishing & Enterprises, LLC
127 E. Trade Center Terrace | Mustang, Oklahoma 73064 USA
1.888.361.9473 | www.tatepublishing.com

Tate Publishing is committed to excellence in the publishing industry. The company reflects the philosophy established by the founders, based on Psalm 68:11,
"The Lord gave the word and great was the company of those who published it."

Book design copyright © 2014 by Tate Publishing, LLC. All rights reserved.
Cover design by Gian Philipp Rufin
Interior design by Mary Jean Archival

Published in the United States of America

ISBN: 978-1-63418-821-0
1. Family & Relationships / Marriage & Long Term Relationships
2. Self-Help / Communication & Social Skills
14.11.07

To the three important people in my life: God; my mother, Willie Mae Hitchens; and my wife, Stella Hitchens.

To God, I thank you because you loved me enough to allow me to go through all I had to go through to be the person I am today.

To my mom, who has gone on to be with the Lord, I want to thank you for being a big part of my life in every way. I often think about you and smile to myself wondering, what would you have said if you were still with me?

And last but not least, the person who inspired me to write this book in the first place, my wife, a great woman of God. You have shown extraordinary patience, strength, and courage in our marriage. I'm extremely proud that you would even give me the honor of being your husband. You're my best friend in the world, and I wouldn't have it any other way. You have truly been a blessing to me, even through sickness and in health, without wavering. You're an awesome wife and mother, as well as a great friend to those in need. You have shown time and time again that you will not give up on me even when I had given up on myself. You prayed for me when I couldn't pray for myself. You also gave me a chance to redeem myself as a man and as a husband, and for that I say, thank you, and I love you.

Contents

Prayer

I pray that God will bless every person and every marriage that lay their eyes upon the words in this book, because He gave me the wisdom and the knowledge to write it. I pray that no weapon formed against your marriage shall prosper. I hope your marriage and marriages across the world will be blessed beyond every figment of my imagination. In Jesus's name. Amen.

To God be the glory.

Marriage Statistics

According to the United States of America Census Bureau, the divorce rate in America is:

41%–50% in first marriages
60%–70% in second marriages
73%–74% in third marriages

These were some eye opening stats to me because my thinking was the complete opposite of what this chart shows. I would have thought that the percentages would have been lower as the times of marriage grew, but as you can see that's not the case. As I stared at this chart I began to think "Wow". Then it hit me as I was thinking on this, the reason I believe the percentage climbed is the very reason I wrote this book. Most people leave their marriage pointing fingers at the person they were married to and not taking the responsibility for their short comings. So instead of taking the time to focus on themselves and begin examining what was wrong within them, they go and get someone new and keep their old ways. This, by looking at this chart, is not working!

The days of you deciding to throw away what you have and getting someone else is not a good choice based on this chart. Here's another chilling fact about marriages from the U.S. Census Bureau:

Marriages that include children of divorced parents are prone to divorcing 4 times more than the children of couples who are not divorced.

This statistic to me sounds like something hereditary that can be passed down from generation to generation if you're not careful. If this was part of you or your spouse's heritage, make it your business not to add to this statistic! Just know statistic can be overcome, that's why you very rarely see 100% statistics, because there are always people who can beat the odds even when they are stacked against them. This could be your marriage, so get past the odds and accept the challenge and "Begin the Search: Finding Your Marriage One Phase at a Time."

Introduction

This book consists of three different phases that will challenge your marriage in different ways; some may be more difficult to handle than others, but they are all part of the marriage search process. If you feel that a particular topic discussed in a phase does not pertain to you, I suggest reading it anyway; this could possibly help avoid some potential bumps in the future.

It is my hope that you both will give each topic the time and the attention that it deserves to properly complete the challenges that it presents to you and your spouse before entering into the next topic. This is not a race against time; this is simply a change in direction. Get out the mind-set of "My marriage is over" and get in to the mind-set of "My marriage is just about to start."

Both of you deserve to be happy, so don't give in to the world's way of marriage by throwing in the towel when times get rough, but strap on God's way and keep moving forward and believing every day is a new day and a new beginning. Roll up your sleeves and your pant legs and get ready to go to work for something everybody wishes they had at some point in their life, "a great marriage."

Remember these two words as you begin your quest to a great marriage: *love* and *respect*.

Foundation

In order to build anything solid, it must first have a solid foundation. When I think of solid, I think of the almighty, never-wavering God. He to me represents the true definition of solid, so when you include him in the core of your relationship, it's already headed in the right direction. He created us and formed us into his most prized creation of all, and he told us in scripture what it would take to satisfy us, what we like and don't like, what a man's needs are, and the needs of a woman. Our job in this is to equip ourselves with this knowledge and execute to the best of our ability. In Ephesians 5:31–33 (NLT), He draws a simple blueprint on marriage"

> A man leaves his father and mother and is joined to his wife, and the two are united into one. This is great mystery, but it is an illustration of the way Christ and the church are one. So again I say, each man must *LOVE* his wife as he loves himself, the wife must *RESPECT* her husband [emphasis mine].

As you can see, God has set the foundation for marriage and has given responsibilities to each partner in this verse of the Bible. Now, we need to embrace these principles as we move forward in the book. Keep your mind and your heart on the foundation of marriage and its duties that we have as voluntary participants in this lifelong partnership. Love and respect are two critical things that God has assigned to us. Before you got married, you probably thought this would be easy to handle. But when two more challenging words, *trial* and *tribulation*, come against you, it then becomes even more difficult to sustain those responsibilities, and most marriages don't make it through.

Open up yourself to the words within these pages that you are about to read, allowing yourself to feel uncomfortable, guilty, irritated, or even sad at times; it's okay. Because after all of the soul-searching you and your spouse have to do to find yourselves individually, just know when the search is over, you both will have found "your marriage."

Warning

This book is not very long, as you can see from flipping through the pages, and there is a reason for that. I prefer to not have all your time spent reading about how to fix your marriage; I would rather you spend time actually enjoying being married instead. Life is too short not to enjoy every day with the person you love.

Phase I

This first phase will be the most important part of them all, simply because here is where all of the junk is being dealt with and laid out on the table. You will also have a chance to discuss things that has changed now that you are married. You are going to be able to deal with the hurt and pain you may have been hiding underneath a fake smile in front of friends and family. This is now the time to put on your rubber boots so that you can really dig in and uproot all the feelings that have been buried over the years. Don't be ashamed to let go and share what's going on inside of you on a daily basis because it will only get you to where you need to be in your marriage.

It's important to have a vehicle that you can attach yourself to in order to release the stress of marriage that can accumulate unintentionally and unexpectedly over a period of time in your relationship. The problem is not the problem itself, but in most cases, it's the not dealing with the problem that's really the problem, as you well know. What I have found in my own marriage, even when I knew the consequence of my actions, I continued to not make the necessary corrections to fix the problem. Why is that? In most cases, we become complacent in our marriages, and we a lot of times tend to forget the answer to these important questions.

A. Why did we get married? (Because we fell in love)
B. Who did we marry? (A very good person who we want to spend the rest of our life with)
C. Last but not least, the covenant before God that we committed to (you know, through the good and the bad, in sickness and in health, until death do you part—yeah, that)

I believe within these pages holds the key to that vehicle your marriage has been longing for, for I don't know how long, but I'm sure you and your spouse know exactly how long it's been. Your marriage is obviously very important to you and to your spouse if you're reading this book, so don't take it lightly (I recommend you read this together, but if not, as long as you both read it). I want you both to really tune in on the "you part of this book; if you both can do this, this will be the saving grace of your marriage. What I mean about the "you" part is that a lot of time we tend to play the blame game when we read books like this. But I challenge you and your spouse to keep the focus on the area within yourself that needs to be worked on and to help each other in the place you both fall short.

Let's not forget we are on the same team; oftentimes we forget that, and our marriage suffers because we are so busy fighting against each other instead of working together. As you know, our fight is never against flesh and blood but against spirits and principalities. I believe we should use this valuable information to defuse situations that entice us to fight against flesh and blood in our marriage.

As you begin to read these pages, the purpose is to create a mirror effect that will begin to change what you see in yourself and your marriage. So keep your heart, your mind, and your soul open to change, and embrace the changes with all the love that you have for each other.

Communication

Communication is the key in all relationships, especially marriage, as we all know. We've heard it time and time again, from every source and book since the beginning of time. So to me if something is written and talked about that many times, *it must be true*! All throughout the Bible, God was communicating through many different people and even animals (Numbers 22:26–34, NLT); he also spoke using a burning bush to get his message into the earth. Jesus himself walked the earth casting out demons and calming the seas and the winds through a profound and powerful way of communication by just speaking to them. Here's a great scripture to look at in the Bible where God shows his power through the Word and the power of words.

> In the beginning the Word already existed. The Word was with God and the Word was God. He existed in the beginning with God. God created everything through him, and nothing was created except through him. The Word gave life to everything that was created, and his life brought light to everyone. (John 1:1–4, NLT)

As you can see, not only is God showing us the power of the Word of God, but just the terminology that he uses in doing so are astonishing. He calls the words *he*, saying "he existed." God uses words in the form of a person. He also goes on to say, "Nothing was created except through him." The power of words became unbelievable to me when I read this text. Words created our very existence, so don't underestimate the power that communication could have in your marriage. Use words positively rather than negatively as these positive conversations will prove beneficial in your marriage.

Talking is totally different from communication in that it can be done with no involvement from another person. Communication is talking that involves both parties engaged in a meaningful or meaningless conversation, but as long as both parties are participating. Beneficial communication is what I believe is vital in a marriage. You may be thinking, *Well, what is beneficial communication?* There are a few different beneficial ways to communicate, like emotional (speaking to their emotional side; some call it love language), touching, and hugging (a showing of affection.) Verbal communication is very important. This is the best way for us to let the person (who is in this marriage with us, by the way) know what's going on inside of us.

Communication has to be established and accessible when it's time to reveal the inside of us into the atmosphere of your marriage. One thing you must not do is expect your partner to figure it out for themselves; it's not fair, and it does not work all the time. The only thing that's foolproof is having an open door policy when it comes to communication in your marriage. Especially if it's something that is bothering you, the enemy will have a field day in your mind if what's wrong is not brought to the table for discussion. Guess what? Your spouse should be the one you open up to when that time comes in your marriage because that's when the relationship grows. I believe there is no better time to express your love to the person you love than through intimate conversations. This moment of communication could take your marriage to another level faster than a blink of an eye.

Believe it or not, the person you married wants to talk, have pillow fights with you, and laugh at your not-so-funny jokes as well as hug and kiss you too. These are all ways of beneficial communications that can really electrify your relationship. It's okay to be in a marriage and have a friendship as well; as a matter a fact, that's probably what you are both missing the most about how your relationship used to be.

I myself like the love language part about relationships. This is where you sync in on what they enjoy the most that you do for him/her, and they can't help but love you more every time you do it. For my wife, it's flowers; any kind of fresh flowers will do (as long as they are alive, of course), and she is as happy as can be. Because I know that's her love language, I feed that love often. Here's a question: do you know your spouse's love language? And do they know yours? If not, I suggest you both talk about it together; this should not be a secret. Make it fun; don't get mad if they don't know what it is already, just be thankful that you're talking about it.

The best thing about a conversation is it takes little or no effort to start one up; it could be something a friend or a coworker may have had a question about, and you just want a different opinion on the matter. You never know, your spouse may have an insight on the topic that you may not have thought of that could be helpful to that particular person. I do not promote opposite sex relationships outside of the workplace unless both parties are helping to solve a problem.) Now, as I was saying, don't shut each other out; it's okay to say what you thought was funny or what you may think your spouse thinks is funny. It's okay to *live* in your marriage. The day isn't over because you came home from work; it's just beginning.

Wow, what a wonderful day it will be when *conversation* won't seem like work but a refreshing vacation. Always remember, think about your marriage on purpose, not by accident. If taking the first step is saying what's bothering you, then *get it over with*. Your spouse wants it out so that they can enjoy conversations with you again. Keep the lines free from the overwhelming sounds of silence that stems from holding it all in, and instead embrace the clear sounds of conversation and laughter in your marriage.

Now that we have established that communication is the key ingredient in any relationship, let's build on that momentum going forward in this book. Get it in your mind that your marriage depends on how well you communicate with each other and that you're in this together as one. By really grabbing hold of this topic, it will make it a little easier to overcome the rest.

Discussion: Is talking to your husband or wife hard? If so, why? Could it be that you feel they don't listen, or maybe not as attentive as you would like? Or is it that you feel you have nothing in common, and over the years or months, you have grown apart? Maybe they hurt you in the past and never apologized.

Write down your thoughts and feelings separately from each other and compare your thoughts after you've written them down. Be truthful about your thoughts, it's imperative that you start off by establishing communication. Remember, friendship will follow when communication starts.

Husband

_____

_____

_____

_____

_____

_____

_____

_____

_____

_____

_____

_____

_____

_____

_____

_____

_____

_____

_____

_____

_____

_____

_____

_____

Wife

_____

_____

_____

_____

_____

_____

_____

_____

_____

_____

_____

_____

_____

_____

_____

_____

_____

_____

_____

_____

_____

_____

_____

Do You Know Who You Married?

I know you're probably wondering, *What does he mean do I know who I married?* Of course I know who I married (with your head shifting and your fingers snapping). But what you're probably thinking is not what I'm saying. What I am talking about is that do you know the issues, if any, that your spouse has had early on in their life that maybe never was discussed or brought up before in your dating relationship? Things like the following:

1. Being fatherless really did bother him, and he didn't realize how much it did.
2. She may have been sexually molested as a child and never talked about it with anyone because it's embarrassing or because of the fear of not being normal.
3. He may not have been shown how to handle the pressure that comes with being a husband in some areas.
4. She never had mother figures around her to show her how to be a wife and a mother and the balance it takes to keep it all together.

5. Did you deal with the issues that caused your past relationship or relationships to fail?

6. Are you angry at your life and the way it turned out and never dealt with the disappointment that you feel sometimes?

7. Are you angry at someone in your past and never forgave him/her in your heart?

8. What type of childhood did you have? And was it a happy one?

This is what I mean when I posed the question "Do you know who you married?" If for some reason you do not know the answers to these questions about the person you married, then the answer should be no. And it's nothing to be ashamed of; it could simply be that they may have believed that this particular part of their life was over, and they were okay with it. But what I have found—and I'm using my own life as an example—is that these feelings only come out when there sparked by certain situations in life. What follows is an example.

My wife and I were going through a financial trial in our marriage I was feeling less than a man in this area because of the lack of money I had at that time. What happened was I blamed my father for not showing me how to be a responsible man in this area of my life, and I didn't like how I was feeling at all. I thought I was over this feeling I had for him. This feeling sparked me to think of all the other things I was still angry about with him and covered up over the years.

Thank God as soon as my wife realized what was going on with me and that this was more than just about the bills, she immediately put me in the car and drove me to the three huge crosses (out front of the church), and I let it all out. Wow, I didn't know how much I was still hurting, but thank God that he was able to use my wife as an outlet when I needed it the most. I was able to truly forgive my father for the first time, and more importantly, I know now that he only did what he knew how to do, and I'm good with that now. Now it's my turn to make a change with my family.

Maybe something similar is going on with you, and you would love to be able to release all of the hurt that's causing problems with your marriage. I urge you both to have this conversation with each other just as reassurances that everything is out and nothing is weighing you down emotionally. Remember, there are questions we will never know the answers to unless someone asks it.

I hope my life's example has been of help to opening up the window that the wind may have closed by mistake. Now it's time to close it yourself for good.

Discussion: Short but *very serious* topic. This topic was written to get both of you to do a *self-check* into your past and to reveal anything that is not as *overcome* as you thought.

Now it's time to share this issue you have with your husband/wife. If you're angry all the time and you don't know why, you may have some "unforgivingness" in your heart, or some hidden hurt from past relationships that's still unresolved. Pray about this together and ask God to heal these old wounds. (Seek further assistance depending on the situation).

Husband

_____
_____
_____
_____
_____
_____
_____
_____
_____
_____
_____
_____
_____
_____
_____
_____
_____
_____
_____
_____
_____
_____

Wife

_____

_____

_____

_____

_____

_____

_____

_____

_____

_____

_____

_____

_____

_____

_____

_____

_____

_____

_____

_____

_____

_____

I Want Who I Married

Before you get married or even before you even meet someone you want to marry, you already have in your mind what type of person you want to spend the rest of your life with. We've all envisioned ourselves being happy with someone you can be yourself with, laugh with, and raise a family with. You had all these wonderful thoughts, then you meet someone who fits or comes close to everything that you have envisioned, and you think this may be "the one." So she tells her girlfriends about you, and you tell your friends about her, and both sets of friends finally get to meet this person and feel that this may be the right person for you as well.

Now that you have the approval we sometimes need from our friends and family, the relationship goes on. You are shown more and more that this is something, or should I say someone, special. "He opens my door for me, and we have the same ideas. He also listens when I talk," she says. "She's beautiful, sexy, she shows support, and she understands me. This is it," he said. You like her family, she likes your family, everybody is so happy that you're finally happy.

Then months pass, no big fights, just a couple of misunderstandings because you're still getting to really know each other, no big deal. Then a year or two passes, and still nothing major happens in the relationship, so now it's time to go to the "big stage." It's time to pop the question: "Will you marry me?" She said, "*Yes.*" She calls up everyone she knows to share this great news: "I'm getting married!" What a feeling as a man; you've just made the woman you love so very happy, and your future together is looking very bright. The engagement stage of the relationship is going great, and you're loving each other more and more with each day that passes.

Now the big day has come, you had a beautiful wedding, life is great, this is on its way to being a great decision that you made. You think to yourself, *I don't know why couples are getting divorced after going through all of this?*

"I married a beautiful woman. We can have sex like crazy, and I don't even have to burn in hell doing so because we are married, and oh yeah, no more flowers or opening doors," he says to himself.

"No more dressing up, getting my hair done, and I don't have to clean up as much either," she says to herself.

Now the person you used to have to say good night to and really didn't want to, you don't have to anymore.

Months in your marriage pass, maybe even a few years, and the newness has worn off. Now you start to remember those thoughts you had after you said I do. You know, the "now I don't have to's," that's what I call them, and before you know it, *bam*! As you're driving down the road, or sitting on the side of your bed, or maybe even taking a quiet walk in the park, you say to yourself, "I miss the talks we had, how we used to laugh and have fun together. Simply put, I want who I married."

What happens to the person we marry? Do we marry them, and they disappear into thin air? Or maybe they have an evil twin we don't know about. Or maybe they put so much energy into getting a spouse that they don't have enough left to put into the marriage. Here's what I believe happens in some cases. Maybe the person you married was who they "wanted" to be then, but couldn't sustain it because he or she hasn't grown into that person just yet. But the good news is that they have the potential to become that person permanently with a little help from you. (I also want to add that if you married while you were young, you really have to be patient in this stage of your marriage with you both having so much room to grow, so be patient with each other).

Because marriage is such a huge commitment, it tends to attract a lot of stress, and the first thing most people do when they get stressed is to give up. Why is that? I believe that it is because stress wears you down, and to get rid of it, we are taught to stop doing whatever it is that stresses us out or get away from it for a while. That may be true for a job or a sport, but not for a marriage or a family because time apart when things are bad is not a good idea. I believe the enemy wouldn't love anything better than to separate the marriage, so separation is not an option (unless it's abusive).

In a marriage that seems to be going downhill, digging in and fighting back will lessen the stress because you're not sitting back watching your marriage fall apart (that's were all the stress comes from). Get involved in your marriage. Don't just sit around, idle, watching the enemy devour your marriage. Get back in the ring and fight like never before.

The enemy is so crafty he will have you thinking all kinds of things that will have you second-guessing your spouse and your marriage, but you need to tell him and mean it: "I want who I married back!" Now you're ready to fight. His purpose is to kill, steal, and destroy, the Bible tells us. We have to know our opponent just as well as he knows us if we stand a chance to win any fight. (And yes, you are in a fight, for those of you who didn't know it.)

Now that you know the person you married is still in there, no matter how it looks on the outside, there's a good person on the inside because you married them. If there wasn't, you wouldn't have married him or her in the first place, so start there. Put God first, and don't give up before the fight begins, and please don't wait for your spouse to start; jump in and start swinging. Believe me, they will join in eventually. Just don't stop swinging.

Discussion: If you feel like you have been the victim of identity theft in your marriage, you're not alone. You can overcome this by telling your husband/wife what you miss about them and what you miss that they used to do for you.

I want you both to write down what each of you miss that your husband/wife used to do. Make a commitment to each other to include these *must-haves* back into your marriage.

Remember: It's not that they don't love you, it may be that they did not know the ramifications of all of the demands that this commitment has to offer. Just give them time to grow in this demanding position that they have embarked upon.

Husband

_____

_____

_____

_____

_____

_____

_____

_____

_____

_____

_____

_____

_____

_____

_____

_____

_____

_____

_____

_____

_____

_____

_____

Wife

_____

_____

_____

_____

_____

_____

_____

_____

_____

_____

_____

_____

_____

_____

_____

_____

_____

_____

_____

_____

_____

_____

_____

_____

_____

_____

The Person You Married
Is Still in There

Life has a way of tossing you and turning you like a frantic sea at times, and it is easy for your marriage to get lost in the day-to-day waves of life. Between work, bills, and kids (if you have them), trying to get into your purpose and plan that God has for you can take a toll on your relationship. But I have found that God has to be the center of it all no matter what is going on around you. Put your marriage right underneath him, and let him carry you both through the distractions of life that covers the love you have for one another.

Your spouse can easily get distracted and not even know it; you have to purposely think about your marriage. The phrase "purposely think about your marriage" is something that should stick in your mind throughout this journey. I truly believe that "the person you married is still in there." How does he know? (You may be saying this to yourself.) Well, I was the one in my marriage feeling like it was over and there's no hope. I guess at some point, when you feel like the life has been sucked out of your marriage, it's a common thought most of time. In my situation, my wife had to pull her husband back out of me, and she did by continuously being loving and kind, no matter how much crap I put out there. In other words, I was complaining about everything, and she was just killing me with kindness. I laugh about it now, but at the time it was so annoying.

I remember being at work, and I would be in one of my moods about something I'm not happy about, whether it would be something in life or something in my marriage, it didn't matter, but I'm sure whatever it was, it didn't make much sense at all. Anyway, my wife asked me what I wanted for dinner one night, and I rudely said, "I don't know." I also remember after I would get off the phone, I would think, *I hate when she does that, always acting like nothing is going on.* But to her, nothing of substance was going on; it was me making thing worse than they actually were. You may be in a situation like that right now in your marriage where you're mad for something that is really nothing. If that's you and you're mad for some reason that doesn't make any sense, *now* is the time to look them in the face and say, "I'm sorry." Because we have to allow our spouses to pull us out of the pit. Stop pushing the rope of love out your way. I often think about this verse in the bible where it says, "If your enemies hungry give them food to eat. If they are thirsty, give them something to drink. In doing this, you will heap burning coals of shame on their heads" (Romans 12:20, NLT).

As you can see from this scripture, kindness is meant to defuse the tension between good and evil. When you're in a marriage, someone has to be the bigger person because both of you at some point will experience being the one in the pit and needing the rope of love to be thrown down to them, so don't push it away; grab it and start climbing out. The person you married is still in there! Don't allow pride to dictate the success of your marriage anymore.

My wife had her time in the pit as well—our finances were in terrible trouble, we had just gotten married, and we were struggling. The enemy was hitting us from all sides, and the ship of love was sinking fast. My wife was really not good with this at all, but in this particular time in our marriage, I was the one looking over the whole of life, and I had to throw her the rope of love. Do you see how it works? God always leaves us a way out of these times in our marriage and even in our lives. The way I see it, as long as one of you is on solid ground, God will all ways provide the rope. Because "the person you married is still in there."

Discussion: Are you guilty of giving too much time to a ridiculous argument and you don't know how to let it go? You have to stop allowing the enemy to steal your time over nonsense that has no barring in your marriage.

Write down a decree to each other that states that a disagreement will not go hours and definitely not overnight without someone pulling the other out of the pit.

Husband

_____

_____

_____

_____

_____

_____

_____

_____

_____

_____

_____

_____

_____

_____

_____

_____

_____

_____

_____

_____

_____

_____

Wife

_____

_____

_____

_____

_____

_____

_____

_____

_____

_____

_____

_____

_____

_____

_____

_____

_____

_____

_____

_____

_____

Stop

Please, please, please, don't rush into phase 2. Take all the time you need to digest all the information you have read in the previous topics. I want you to take time out to deal with the issues that are at hand. Don't sweep anything under the rug; lay it all out on the table, and expose the enemy for who and what he really is, a failure and a liar, and now I believe he has failed again.

Make sure that a clear line of communication has been well established in your marriage; take on the tough issues of infidelity, lies, unhappiness, disappointment, disrespect, lack of love, and deception. But do it all in *love* and in *respect*. Keep in mind that you're reading this book for a reason and know that it sometimes takes *forgiveness* and *understanding* to save your marriage when love is covered by junk.

See you in phase 2, where I'm going to continue to challenge both of you to go even deeper to find your marriage.

God bless.

Phase II

If you are reading this phase of the book, it means that both of you have identified the issues and have talked them out between yourselves, or may have even gotten some help from an outside source. I hope that you've left no stone unturned, and every secret has been discussed. Because if you have not fully dealt with the issues that started the depletion of your marriage in the first place, then it will be difficult to exercise the practices that are in the next phase.

In this phase, I need both of you to let yourselves go with each other even more. You should feel a lot more relaxed than you did in the beginning. Even though there's still more work to be done to get your marriage to the level I'm sure you're both hoping for, I hope that all the issues in the first phase are now *defeated*. Both of you hopefully have come to grips with the fact that the enemy has stolen enough of your time with childish behavior and useless arguments. Think about this for a moment. The time that you've wasted can never be given back, so get the fire and passion back that you still have for each other and enjoy your life together.

It's time you take control of your marriage and the people surrounding it. It's also time to begin giving your partner more of what they need, and that's the love that convinced you to marry them in the first place. After going through phase 1, you should be more equipped to handle conversation better and more mature in areas you may have lacked maturity and understanding in before. I love this scripture Paul wrote in 1 Corinthians 13:11 (NLT). It's simple and profound at the same time:

> When I was a child, I spoke and thought like a child and reasoned as a child. But when I grew up, I put away childish things.

Now is our time to grow up in our relationship and continue to put behind our selfish behavior as well as the "stinkin' thinkin'" and turn this relationship into an awesome marriage.

Continue to talk your way through to a great marriage in this next set of topics, and do it all in *love* and *respect* for each other. Remember, "it's not about you, it's about your marriage."

Friends in Marriage

I knew when I decided to write on this topic it was going to be a little painful at the beginning, but I will soften the blow at the end.

It's our job to decipher what level of topic we should include friends or, for that matter, our own family in for the sake of our marriage. Make up your mind to abort the negative conversation that can poison your thinking toward your husband/wife. Once they get a bad feeling about the one you love, it's hard to change their minds back to what it used to be, before they were involved in your marriage.

We tend to include them because they are the ones that have been there through the good and the bad, the ups and the downs. They are there when we need them for advice in our relationships before we get married. They give advice on our wardrobes, our hair, and in some cases, which direction to go in our career as well. And in some decisions they've been right on, but in other decisions they've been right off (if you know what I mean). But we still love them because they mean the best for us at the end of the day. So we keep them in tune and plugged into our lives and our day-to-day life.

Now, let's discuss friends in a marriage setting and see if the friendship you have now line up with the caliber of relationship that you are in now, which a marriage is. You see, having a friend in a typical dating type of setting or even a boyfriend-girlfriend relationship requires different levels of friendship. I believe that the friendship has to grow with the level of relationship that you are in, in your life. You cannot allow your friend's dating or boyfriend-girlfriend state of mind to influence a marriage-level relationship.

Let's go a little more into what I mean when I say marriage level. Okay, marriage is tied to a higher power—God. Our marriage is attached to him because we took an oath that included him, or should I say invited him into our marriage. And in that oath, we say, "Until death do us part." Now to me, that's serious business, and it shows the level of relationship that we now have in our life. No dating situation or boyfriend-girlfriend type relationship carries that kind of weight. Why? Because marriage is more than a relationship; it's a *commitment*! That means you don't leave at the first sign of trouble or second, third, fourth, or fifth time either. Why? Because you're in *commitment*! Now, ask yourself this. Do your friends' level of advice at this present time line up with the level of relationship you are in right now? If not, then you need to reevaluate the advice they are giving you *immediately*.

Now, when I say reevaluate, it simply means that depending on what type of feedback that they are giving you when you inquire about what you should do in certain situations, are they telling you things like "I wouldn't forgive him/her if I were you," or maybe things like "You can do bad by yourself," and "You should just leave if you're not happy." If you're hearing this or anything close to this, then don't listen! This is a sign that you may not want to pursue their advice at this time or stage of your marriage. This is the time where you have to start X-ing out some of the people and some of the advice-giving of your struggles in your marriage. This type of advice is on the dating level, not the marriage level; it's important that we guard against this type of negative conversation when trying to save our marriage. Let me be perfectly clear: I am not telling you to dump them as friends, but I am saying be careful of the advice you get no matter if it's family or friends because in the end, it's your marriage, not theirs.

If you feel as if the walls are closing in on you, run to God first, not your friends, for comfort. He is the best comforter there is, and the comfort that He provides will also renew your strength in your current trial. It's okay to get help from a source other than friends if they are always making negative comments every time you confide in them, but God is your best source. All the negative advice is doing is just beating up on what's already a painful and heartbreaking moment in your life; it's also cracking the foundation of your marriage. Whatever you do, don't allow friends or family members and life's growing pains twist the knife in the back of your marriage and make you lose someone you forgot you still love.

A troubled marriage has the ability to attract "unintentional friends" as well as break up long-term friends. What is an unintentional friend (friends of the opposite sex friends)? My definition of an unintentional friend is someone you talk to but have no intentions on being friends at all with this person, but they have hidden intent on being your friend and more if you're not careful. Now it's important to know where this type of person will most likely approach you. So you can be aware or alert when this type of person offers their "friendship." They are in just about every grocery store frozen-food section, mall, at every checkout counter, while you're at the gas station, waiting just for the right moment to pop the two big questions (and not one of them are not, "Will you marry me?" You're already married!). It's "Are you married?" and "Are you happily married?" If you give the wrong answers to either question, then you have now opened the door to an unintentional friend, and now it's on.

What happens at this point, most of the time is you feel you can't talk to your spouse, so now you will have someone to talk to when they're not around. You began to make excuses for something you know is not right. "Since I can't talk to my friends about this, it will be nice to get an opinion from someone who's not close to either of us. This could be good for my marriage." *Wrong! This is one of the worst things you could ever do in a marriage!* You cannot start talking to someone of the opposite sex in stores, on the phone, or even have lunch by yourself with them and discuss the struggles of your marriage or anything else for that matter. Got it? This is not an option, so if you're doing it, *end it today, not tomorrow!* This will in no way help your marriage.

Sometimes we have to ask ourselves questions before we do things that will impact someone else's life. Questions like, how would I feel if my wife/husband did that to me? Or how will my kids or family feel if I go through with this? I have been guilty of making that decision by reacting and not thinking myself, and maybe you have too. But it's not too late to get the compassion back that stops the outside static from destroying your marriage. With a little patience, we could be listening to the smooth sounds of love on our own original station again, but this time in *high definition* instead of trying to find a new station with hidden agenda.

We reach outside of our marriage to others a lot of times because we're not friends with our partner. To communicate is one thing, but being friends is an entirely different stage. Someone may be thinking, how do we become friends? I suggest to anyone you should be best friends before you get married, but if you didn't, it's not too late. I believe becoming friends can be established when two people go through something together that builds a bond. This is most of the time a struggle in your life by which this person has been there for you through it all. You may be reading this book with the person who has been there for you (I hope so), because in most marriages, we have struggles, and once these struggles are over, they could make a statement of friendship in our marriage if we decide to stick it out. (It did for my marriage.) If my wife and I weren't friends, we probably wouldn't be together today.

Giving in to the desire to be married to your best friend can alleviate some of the outside interference that will sometimes confuse your thinking and your emotions. Being friends in a marriage setting will astronomically exalt your marriage to a place that you will have never imagined a relationship could go, and it could be the saving grace of it. If trouble comes your way, having friendship as part of your foundation will make talking easier and constructive criticism less painful to accept than before. Communication is the key, as we discussed in the beginning; but when you add the friendship aspect to it, it becomes electric.

Don't leave this topic until you have both established the fact that *you are friends* or desperately want to be friends, because the next few topics are depending on the ability of your *communication* and *friendship* in order to reach its full potential, and that being "Friends in Marriage."

There is so much more I could say about this, but I hope you've gotten the point. You don't need an outside source in your marriage tearing it down. Just put God in the center of the ring with you and surround yourself with positive friends who are going to encourage you and pray for your marriage. I truly believe that what the devil meant for bad, God will make it awesome!

Discussion: Wow! What a topic, a lot to take in, right? But here's what I would like both of you to do: when you write this, be very careful not to keep this information lying around; it could get misconstrued.

I'd like both of you to evaluate your friends and your loved ones using the headers *Positive* and *Negative* based on their advice in your marriage. Then write another list using the headers *Married* and *Not Married*.

When you finish, you should be able to distinguish between who you can talk to and who may not be the right person to get advice from about a *marriage level* issue. Becoming best friends should be a passion to conquer if not conquered already; and if you're involved with someone of the opposite sex and you consider them a friend and your husband/wife has no idea that this is going on, nor do they know the person, no matter how innocent it is, end it *now*!

Husband

_____

_____

_____

_____

_____

_____

_____

_____

_____

_____

_____

_____

_____

_____

_____

_____

_____

_____

_____

_____

_____

Wife

The Importance of Visualization

I guess this first paragraph would be consideration an introduction to this topic. I want to do my best to make you both feel comfortable before I get started.

I thought long and hard about where to place this topic in the book. I consulted my wife about it, and I still wasn't sure, but she made some valid points. So I thought to myself, *You better be able to talk to each other in order to say what you like for them to change about them, right?* and it better be executed with love and respect for sure, *especially men to their wives,* I said, laughing to myself. So if you have taken the first phase of this and the topic before this one seriously as you should have, so now if your spouse wants to give some constructive observations and suggestions of what they like and miss, embrace it. Remember it's coming from the one you love and who loves you. And, husbands, this is not all about the wife, we have issues in this area as well and you know that it's all said and done in love. Allow each other to be honest and keep open communication at all times during this topic as you have learned to do in previous topics.

Let's rewind to the beginning, if you will. He saw you from a distance or maybe you saw him first, but most likely it was some type of visual display. I know what most of you are thinking right now. "Looks don't matter," or "It's what's on the inside that counts," or "It's about *love*." And that's all true, but let's be really honest with ourselves; appearance plays a big part in whether we are going to date someone or not. Why is that? Because when we meet someone that we don't know, we can't see the inside of that person, so until we get to know him/her, their visual presentation, or lack thereof, will have to do for now.

One thing I know, when you meet someone for the first time, we focus more on our appearance than anything else. We don't want them to see anything wrong with our physical appearance. Why? Because *it matters*! Say it with me.

> My appearance mattered before we got married, and now that we're married, it matters even more!

So don't think for one second that you can just let yourself go when you get married, and everything is fine; it doesn't work like that, sorry. That selfish way of thinking alone has brought a lot of marriages to a screeching halt, and you wonder why. It's amazing how quickly we forget the very thing that caught our attention in the beginning of this relationship.

I have found that the best thing you can do for your marriage is to not lose focus on the importance of the visual aspect in your marriage. We can't afford to let our guard down in any area because as soon as the enemy thinks that we have gotten comfortable, we become vulnerable. And that's not good for you or your spouse. Why? Because the enemy has a way of showing us things that make us lose focus on the *blessing* that we have right in front of us. For example, television—this is one of the most destructive tools ever invented when your focus is not in the right place. I want you to break this word down with me and let's see what it means. Tel-e-vi-sion. Now say it slowly. When I say it slow, what comes to my mind is "tell me a vision." That's powerful, the TV is telling you a vision. Wow!

Now, I hope you see what this means to your marriage. It's important to your marriage that you *tell each other a vision* because the TV's visions can sometimes steal the view that you once enjoyed. And that's the same false sense of attraction that makes us lust after other people when we are out and about in the public arena of life. Why does your spouse tend to look at another person? I believe they are just missing a visual display that they once enjoyed from you. But guess what? You can have those butterflies that you once had back with just a little hunger and desire for your marriage.

The best place to start is in the comfort of your home. Everything starts at home because this is where we are most comfortable. So when you are home, set the tone of "This is my house," or maybe you may say, "This is my palace." Create an environment that you are the best thing since "corn bread" or maybe that you are the "bomb." Instead of your home having a cold and dry atmosphere with no sense of visual presence, create a vision that will leave a lasting impression on your spouse that they can't get out of their head (it doesn't have to be provocative).

In Genesis 29:16–19 (NLT), Jacob worked for Laban for seven years to be with his daughter, Rachel, and he did it without getting a paycheck. Now why would someone do something like that? It sounds crazy in this day and time to give up seven years of your life to marry someone. But the Bible gives us a glimpse into the mind of Jacob, describing what he saw that gave him the motivation and the courage to even suggest such a thing. Listen to why he did what he did to be with her, and I quote, "Rachel had a beautiful figure and a lovely face." In other words, she was beautiful and fine; how about that for a visual display? I'm sure he wasn't thinking about how long or what he had to do to be with her.

Now ask yourself, "What kind of display am I showing my spouse?" Or "Am I cautious of or even care about this area in my marriage?"

As I continued to read this text in the Bible, it mentions that Rachel had a sister named Leah. She didn't catch the attention of Jacob, obviously, because the Bible said, "She didn't have that *sparkle* in her eyes." When I read that, I immediately thought to myself she was the type that really didn't care about her appearance or had any confidence in herself. In other words, she didn't have *it*. You know, *it*, the thing no one can really explain; you just know when you meet someone, and they have *it*. Leah didn't have it, and Jacob knew that she didn't, and that's why he decided to work for the one who had it.

Looking at this story and applying its implications to a marital perspective, it makes all the sense in the world. We tend to not really care about what we show our spouse; as you can see, visualization plays a critical role in your thinking process and the amount of effort and energy that is abstracted in your marriage. Example, have you ever had a disagreement with your spouse on the phone, and you were upset until you made it home? And when you get home, you're not thinking that the vision you see when you walk through the door will have any impact on how you are feeling, so immediately, all the madness goes away as soon as you set your eyes on him/her. That happens because the attractive vision that was displayed for you canceled all of the wrong thinking that was going on in your mind. I truly believe that when your spouse goes out of their way to exemplify an attractive display for you, something inside of you just starts to really appreciate what you have. Another thing, it doesn't hurt to know that they care enough about you to give you a vision that sparks you to do something for them and your marriage without a thought.

Being mindful of the visual content that you display can help avoid a lot of wrong thinking, thinking that can easily develop over time. Your spouse could easily begin to think that "you don't love them anymore" or maybe "now you've gotten what you wanted, so you don't care anymore." You want to try your best to avoid your spouse from seeing a vision that reveals these thoughts. Because thoughts like these could easily grow into something that could end your marriage. I know you don't want this to be the reason your marriage ends because all it takes is you taking a look at yourself through the eyes of the one you love.

If giving a negative visual display is something you're guilty of in your marriage, then it's not too late to change the vision. We've all lost focus at some point in some area of our marriage. This is an area that's so easily neglected in a marriage because most of the time your spouse doesn't have the courage to say anything to you, but believe me, they're thinking it. This is something that can easily be fixed, so don't *think, react*, and recreate a vision that will put the *spark* back into the eyes of your spouse. This will reap *huge* benefits in your marriage, and you'll be glad you did.

Discussion: This can be a tough topic to discuss without the *friendship* aspect of your marriage. Let me explain: this could be fun if you're friends, but a disaster if you're not. I would like you both to discuss this topic in *love* and *respect*, as I recommend often in these topics.

Discuss with each other why and how you've gotten to this point in your marriage. It could be it just got out of control because of the neglect on your part or lack of compliments and appreciation on their part. Take ownership in this area, look at your husband/wife, and say, "I've not given you the best of me in this important area of our marriage, and I'm going to do my best to make it right."

Write down a starting point to give yourself or yourselves some sense of direction going forward.

Husband

Wife

_____
_____
_____
_____
_____
_____
_____
_____
_____
_____
_____
_____
_____
_____
_____
_____
_____
_____
_____
_____
_____
_____
_____
_____
_____

Confidence Makes a Difference

Confidence should be something you have in your marriage between you and your spouse because it is not only sexy, but it opens doors to a lot of fun in your marriage as well. Having confidence in a home setting is not the same as having it outside of the home. Confidence used in the wrong way can be interpreted as cocky, but when used in the right way, it is necessary for your marriage. It will add an excitement that you are loved by the person that you are in the relationship with and that you can freely show it with your spouse.

In most marriages, there's always one person more confident than the other. Why? Because in most cases, it's the person who is getting the compliments from their partner who are the most confident in the marriage. I want to encourage you, if you are the one in the relationship who is just receiving all the compliments, it's time for you to start lifting up your spouse as well; it's not about you, it's about you marriage.

I am convinced that it is healthy for your marriage that both of you have a certain level of confidence between both of you; this will also give you the courage to try new things without hesitating or feeling embarrassed. Think about it this way: if you had only one half of your body, one arm, one leg etc., it would be very difficult for you to win a race against someone with all of their limbs in place, wouldn't it? It's the same in marriage, when one person is being lifted up and the other is sitting down, you can't possibly win the race, so lift up your partner in marriage as well, and then your marriage will have a fair chance in the race against failed marriages.

Now that we have established the fact that confidence is important, we can now take the necessary steps it takes to be comfortable in your new experiences and adventures that you will be partaking on in your marriage. Be careful to identify the personal insecurities that your spouse may have; that could be a problem if not confronted or discussed in your marriage. So what am I talking about when I say personal insecurities? Well, it may be things like weight gain, which is common in most marriages. But even something like weight gain can easily be conquered when confronted in a positive manner.

If you feel that you are not the confident person you once were because of the size that you are today, then it's time you take a stand and not cheat your spouse out of a happy marriage because of your personal hang-ups; it's not fair to them. I believe going to your spouse and admitting that you are having difficulties in this area will hopefully get you the support you need to get your confidence back on track. This can be done collectively as a team and can even become a springboard for your marriage. So if your spouse comes to you with this problem, be encouraging in this and don't shrug it off as nothing; this is a cry for help, so do your part for the sake of your marriage. It could be more fun than you know.

My wife and I had this issue in our marriage. Before we got married, we worked out individually; the problem came once we were married. We stopped working out altogether, and this was not good for either of us; we both got comfortable. So we both started to gain weight and found out very quickly that we didn't like what we were seeing and, more importantly, how we were feeling (it happens; it's not the end of the world). The visual that was once pleasant took a turn for the worst. Even though it is funny and we laugh when we talk about it with each other now, but at the time it was not so funny. What we started to do was work out together, whether it was doing an exercise tape or just walking or running in the neighborhood. The point of the matter is that we supported each other instead of criticizing one another, and it became a fun time for the both of us without realizing it. To this day we still work out together (and for all the men reading this, this is a good way to score some brownie points as well).

You may be reading this, and you and your spouse don't have time to work out together. I don't want you to feel left out if work and kids provide you less time. When time is something that you both don't have a lot of, you can still make an impact in this area by simply making a conscious decision to change your diet together and support each other in that way by incorporating fun with it. You can make it fun by creating a private weight loss competition between each other on a weekly or biweekly basis. Here are some examples:

> The loser has to do dishes for a week. (Yes, men. Dishes.)
> The winner picks the movie when you go on a date night.
> The loser has to give the winner a massage.
> The loser has to give up control of the remote for a day.

These are just some examples you could use to make it more interesting and more exciting. Feel free to come up with ideas you both can agree on to make it a success.

Another great idea if time is an issue is you can create a ten- or fifteen-minute workout regimen before you jump in the shower or bath. Try to include exercises like jumping jacks, push-ups, squats, and stomach crunches. A nightly routine can make a huge impact over a period of time if you're consistent.

By eating a little better and adding a little exercise in your marriage, you will find that the energy level will increase, and you will be able to give each other the confident spouse you both deserve. Your body is a temple, and you're responsible for guarding it, so do your best to help each other every day to get a little better; you will love the results, and you will love each other more as well.

Discussion: Compliments go a long way, so make this part of your marriage. It doesn't cost a thing, and it's a great way to encourage someone when they've lost their way in a particular area of their life. Great tips were given as well; it's entirely up to you if you want to use my suggestions to make it fun. Feel free to write down some ways you would like to support your partner in this area, if it's an issue for them or both or you. This is all about support, because confidence can be lost and found with the right supporting cast around you. Don't allow the enemy to say something to your partner before you do!

Husband

_____

_____

_____

_____

_____

_____

_____

_____

_____

_____

_____

_____

_____

_____

_____

_____

_____

_____

_____

_____

_____

_____

Wife

_____

_____

_____

_____

_____

_____

_____

_____

_____

_____

_____

_____

_____

_____

_____

_____

_____

_____

_____

_____

_____

_____

_____

_____

_____

_____

_____

_____

_____

_____

_____

_____

_____

_____

_____

_____

_____

_____

_____

_____

_____

_____

_____

_____

_____

_____

_____

_____

Don't Make Excuses

Excuses have been part of our lives and our way of thinking since we were kids. When we're given chores to do around the house, we made up excuses or ways to get out of keeping our responsibility to our parents. Most of us said things like, "I don't feel like it" or "Can I do it later?" The list goes on and on. We have all been guilty of this type of neglect of responsibility in some area in our lives.

We can all recall one of the most memorable and most talked-about excuses, which was when Adam gave God the biggest excuse of all time, which had an unspeakable effect on mankind still to this day. We read in Genesis 3:12 (NLT).

> The man replied, "It was the women you gave me who
> gave me the fruit, and I ate it."

In this text, we read that he made an excuse so ridiculous, it not only put God in what I'm sure was an uncomfortable position as a parent, but Adam used God as the main source for his excuse. Wow! Isn't that familiar? How many times have we blamed God for our bad decisions in our life? Countless times! We still have the mind-set of what Adam had back then because we continue to make up excuses and blame someone else when things don't work out in our favor or just downright fail.

In most marriages, we play the blame game a lot. When we don't feel like giving our marriage the attention that it needs, we make up excuses why we're not doing what we need to do to make it work. Excuse no. 1: "God, I prayed for the right person. This can't be the person for me. You made a mistake." Excuse no. 2: "He/she has changed so much since we got married." These are some common excuses we tend to use to end the marriage because if you notice, neither excuse has anything to do with the person who is saying it.

We have to stop allowing this to happen in our marriage, stop coming up with these excuses, and start recognizing that that's what they are. A simple, easy way of knowing if you're not doing your part in your marriage is by taking a quick inventory daily on yourself to see what you've fed your marriage on that day. Some examples would be the following:

> Did you tell your spouse that you loved them today?
> Did you give him/her a kiss or hug today?
> If you were at work, did you call and check on him/her today?
> Did you create a positive vision for him/her?
> Did you ask him/her how they were feeling today?
> Did you ask him/her if they need anything or if he/she needs to talk?

Did you pray and ask God to cover your spouse and marriage today?

As you can see, if we were to take the responsibility upon ourselves rather than making excuses, we will begin to see our marriage take a turn upward. I believe making a conscious effort to go through a mental checklist in our minds daily will keep our marriage grounded in a place that will prove great results for your marriage.

Put all excuses on the back burner, and make a decision to go all out for your marriage, no matter what your day may be like at work or what's going on with the kids, and keep your marriage in perspective through it all. The best way to get through a bad time or even a bad day is to think about someone other than you and your own problems or situations.

A good example is found in the story or the book of Job. We all know of his struggles and his time of testing and hardship in which most of us could not have endured. As I recall, at the end of that story, it all ended when he began to take the focus off himself and began to pray for others (Job 42:10, NLT). This is something we have to begin to apply in our marriage and even our lives, period. The ability to take the attention off ourselves and think of our spouse or people in general is truly a forgotten strategy to obtaining the rewards we so desperately seek.

This way of life will not be easy to conquer at first. You have to remember this: this part of your marriage has been neglected a lot in most cases, so don't be surprised when days come that won't go particularly well. I've experienced those days in my marriage as well, so it is not and shouldn't be shocking at all. What happens in most cases is that your spouse, when that old mind-set kicks in, it tends to bring more attitude when you confront him/her on anything, especially their visual display more than anything else. This is when all the excuses start to flow in all at once. You are going to get them all, I can promise you.

Here they come: I'm tired! I can't have a day? *I don't feel like it!* You can't love me for me? I just want to be comfortable!

It's amazing how quickly we forget all of what's important when the old mind-set kicks in high gear (the lazy bug). When this happens, it's important not to lose your cool. Continue to stay grounded in what's right; somebody has to hold it all together. Now is the time to start dumping those heaps of coal (coals of love, as I call them) all over their heads like never before, and believe me, they will be quickly convicted. And as mad as they are, they will not be able to resist what's *right*.

We all have an opportunity in this common state of thinking, but applying the simple practices that I discussed earlier in this topic will hopefully begin to offset the thought pattern that has the time to think of these unwanted excuses. In the end, making excuses or just not putting forth the effort (just being lazy) will not be a wise choice for the future of your marriage. Do your best to resist the temptation to give your spouse less of you, and feed the pulsating beat of giving him/her your very best.

Don't make excuses. Make memories.

Discussion: What have you been making excuses about? Write them down and make it plain and simple to yourself. When you look at this list, it may make you realize how selfish you've been when you consider the fact that everything you made an excuse not to do affected the person who's in this marriage with you.

Remember, do the things you're required to do as a husband/wife because it's not about you, it's about your marriage at the end of the day. By doing what you're supposed to do, you will eventually get you what you want from them without asking. Somebody has to start, it may as well be you.

Husband

_____

_____

_____

_____

_____

_____

_____

_____

_____

_____

_____

_____

_____

_____

_____

_____

_____

_____

_____

_____

_____

_____

Wife

_____
_____
_____
_____
_____
_____
_____
_____
_____
_____
_____
_____
_____
_____
_____
_____
_____
_____
_____
_____
_____

Stop

We've discussed a lot of great topics in this phase of the *marriage finding* search. Here's what I want you both to do at this particular point in your search. Go back to the beginning of the book, to the "Foundation" chapter, and reread it. Then start at "Communication" and read all the notes that you made from each topic leading up to this point, separately. I want you both to really meditate on your thoughts concerning each topic. This could take a couple of days or even a week, but don't rush! It's a lot to digest, and it could be overwhelming at some point, depending on how lost your marriage was when you started your search.

After you have both completed this assignment, have an open discussion about each topic; this will give both of you an idea of how much you have grown in each area of your marriage. Be completely honest with each other; you should have by now established the fact that this person loves you and that you love them. If you feel you have not overcome a particular topic or topics, it's okay! Everyone will not get it all together at the same time, so be patient with each other and give each other the allotted amount of time that is necessary to overcome whatever topic that they may still have an issue with. I suggest you both pray over that topic immediately together, and claim *victory* over it without fail. This is not a race, this is serious business, and it should be handled accordingly. You may feel the need to talk to your pastor or a marriage counselor if you haven't already, whatever it takes, *do it*!

On the other hand, if you both feel comfortable with the progress you have made to this point and are ready to move forward, then congratulations! This next and final phase is waiting for you. It took a lot of hard work to get to this point, but seeing the change that has taken place in your marriage, I'm sure you can agree it was well worth it. It's time to enjoy yourselves and what you both have accomplished as a team in your marriage. Take the suggestions that I made as you both read the last few topics and make them your own so your marriage can reach an even higher level!

Phase III

Now, in this final phase of this book, both of you will need to let go of your usual stiff, boring, and maybe even dull personality that you have both grown used to in your marriage. This phase will give you both the opportunity to show a side of yourself that has been buried under life's trials and growing pains. It's time to explore new things about each other and rediscover things that have been forgotten or trampled on in the rat race of life. With all the cards on the table and a lot less weight on your shoulders, hopefully you can begin to create the kind of atmosphere in your marriage that will be exciting and adventurous for the both of you.

This also should be the time in your marriage where you start to really take advantage of your newfound communications aspect of your marriage. Now that the door is wide open, just dive in, and I mean really grab a whole of this vital part of your marriage. It is so important to plant a seed in this area right now and at this time. The Bible speaks about time. Simply put, there is a time for everything, and I believe the time is now for your communication to catapult your marriage into a whole new dimension.

Open your eyes to your marriage and look for the chance to make a lasting impression on your spouse. Be as creative as you want to be. This is *your marriage*; make it something you can be comfortable in and free in. Don't be afraid to take the lead. Cook something you've never cooked before, go places you've never been before; don't even think about it. Just do it.

I'm so excited for your marriage, and I can't wait for all of the letters containing these beautiful stories to start pouring in because this would mean that my obedience has really paid off in the most gratifying way.

Just know that without a test, there would be no testimony. And without a trial, there would be no true victory. And without victory, there would be no praise. Someday you will be able to look back on these struggles and embrace them all because without them, you would still be who you were and not who God created you to be. Now, shake off all the dust that has dimmed the light that once shined on your marriage and release the blinding gleam that's dying to be polished and admired.

Every Night a Saturday

For as long as I can remember, Saturday night has been the most anticipated day of the week, and in most cases, it beats out Sunday (unfortunately). This is the day that majority of our planned activities are made in almost all marriages. Why? Because most the time of the time our week consists of mainly work, kids (if you have kids), and TV (routine).

As my wife and I began this journey of finding our marriage, a thought crossed my mind: *What if we didn't wait until Saturday to do something we wanted to do? What if we decided to break out of the normal routine of planning Saturday night like most people do?*

I began to believe that you don't have to be retired to live and enjoy life. I also think we should not put all of our hopes on one day out of the week and forget about the other six days God has blessed us with (now that does not mean go out every day of the week; it simply means pick another day besides Saturday to do something, that's all). With that in mind, we decided to be more spontaneous and take advantage of all the fun we were missing out by making Saturday our go-to day of the week.

I believe going out to dinner and having a midweek experience can add to that dating mentality in your marriage that we touched on earlier. We really have to grab hold of the acceptance of change and let go of the "going through the motions" mind-set that cripples our marriages. There is nothing in our marital vows that said, "We can no longer go on a date during the week or that we have to only enjoy ourselves on Saturday night," so *stop having a one-day-a-week marriage*!

What we have also found is if you like to shop, by going shopping during the week, it is much more peaceful than on the weekends as well. It's more intimate, and it gives you both the time you need to really think and talk about the items that you are buying. You are also able to shop freely without feeling rushed or bombarded by large crowds of people. By engaging in a different shopping experience, you can focus on what's really important, and that's having fun with the one you love. In my own experience, by changing my shopping experiences with my wife, I am able to really see her without the crowds and the background noise that you would experience on a typical Saturday afternoon. Remember, learning to embrace change will have a lasting effect on your marriage, so welcome it with open arms.

While writing on this topic, I also began to think back to when going and doing anything on a weekday was not an option. The reason was most likely the same exact reason you're thinking right now. Things like the following:

- I worked all day.
- I am tired.
- I don't feel like it.
- Let's wait until the weekend.
- We don't have a babysitter.

Let's not forget the meaning of these little phases. They are *excuses*! And you know what I have to say about them when it comes to something as important as your marriage: *don't make any*! The reason they are excuses is because they're being made only because you're married and not dating. Let's be honest, when we were just dating our spouse, we didn't care what day of the week it was or whether or not we went to work that day. Why? Because we wanted to spend time with them at any cost, that's why. We didn't have to have ten hours of sleep a day like you do when you get married. We were happy if we got four or five hours at the most, right?

Mixing it up and changing from the norm can only improve what you have already started to repair in your marriage. Now, I have only listed two weekly activities, but there are many more you can incorporate in your week. Need I remind you, everything that's open on Saturday is open during the week as well, in case you didn't know it? You can go to your local church for Bible study, bowling, or even catch a movie. If you're the couple that just always goes home and watches TV and never experiences any weekday activity, you are in for a treat. Just from talking to other couples, I was surprised to hear how many people never include any other day of the week into their marital relationship (but we used to be one of those couples as well). But thankfully, we broke out of the norm and started to pick our Saturday from any day of the week.

It's never been a better time to experience the fact that Saturday is not the only Saturday in your week, but any day can be your Saturday, if you're willing change from the normal routine. Please don't forget about all of the hard work that you have put into your marriage to get to this point. So "have fun" in every new endeavor that you decide to embark on going forward. You now have the right to pick your Saturday because you've both earned it. Celebrate every chance you get!

Discussion: This topic is all about planning, planning, planning (especially if you have kids). I challenge you both to get out of the norm and explore a new experience; this is going to be really good for your marriage and your newfound friendship. I believe this activity will bring the dating mentality back into your marriage. Take off the limits and live in your marriage! Try it, pick a day together (other than Saturday), and make that day your Saturday. Write down some activities that you would like to do (but used to make excuses not to do it until Saturday).

Husband

_____

_____

_____

_____

_____

_____

_____

_____

_____

_____

_____

_____

_____

_____

_____

_____

_____

_____

_____

_____

_____

_____

Wife

_____
_____
_____
_____
_____
_____
_____
_____
_____
_____
_____
_____
_____
_____
_____
_____
_____
_____
_____
_____
_____
_____

Having Fun in Marriage

In this day and time that we live in, *fun* and *marriage* are not spoken in the same breath or even used in the same sentence in most cases, but it does exits. What we have to do as married couples is tap into this somehow abandoned area of our marriage that's so incredibly ignored; it's called having fun. Having fun in your marriage is easy once you have gone through the fixation portion of this book and have allowed yourself to be operated on with the words and exercises that have been put before you and your spouse.

I truly believe we are allowing fun to seize the exits in our marriages, and I can assure you it's not on purpose. A lot of times we don't know how to have fun anymore; fun has simply been robbed from our marital relationship altogether. If you were to think back on what made your spouse smile while you were dating, it would probably still have the same effect today.(Don't be afraid to say what you're thinking; it will most likely make them smile, and that's what your aiming for.) A dating relationship should never outdo a marriage. Why do I say that? Because not only do you have a covenant that is given to you by the *Almighty God*, but now you have the person you love with you more than ever, and that should be enough if you ask me.

Let's for a second think back about when you were dating and the feelings you had, the fun you shared, and I mean the effortless fun you had together. All of the late-night conversations and all the attentiveness that was shown when the other person spoke or had something to say, how you wouldn't blink an eye as you were so afraid you might miss something important. What were you doing differently then than what you are doing now? In most cases, nothing, but in some cases you are doing less now because the relationship has gotten older, and now those things that used to be fun are not anymore. Why does this happen? What I'm learning in my own marriage is that the marriage doesn't get old, the marriage matures, and when this happens, we don't mature in it. This simply means that you have to do things differently, bring new ideas and new adventures to the marriage. Time does not just stand still; you can't spend your life or your time wishing things get better. Implement some new activities into your marriage to add a new spin on it. Complacency is boring and shouldn't have a dwelling place in your marriage at all; it will drain the life right out of your relationship. What you need is a spark of fire in your marriage that will eventually grow into a wildfire of fun and new experiences.

Start planning activities neither of you have ever done but would like to do or you think you would enjoy doing. Make an agreement to each other that no matter what each of you come up with, you both have to try it together without complaining or even questioning the activity that your spouse wants to experience. You have to be willing to try new things as a couple without judgment or cutting the other person down with a sour spirit or an unwilling attitude. By putting your own selfish feelings to the side, this could potentially open up something on the inside of you that you didn't know was there, or you maybe just enjoyed the experience yourself, and if that is the case, let your spouse know that you enjoyed it as well.

Here's a list of things to try or add to your relationship:

1. Go out to a new restaurant neither of you have eaten at before. While there, you are to try an entrée that's new to you and have taste test with each other's food and talk about your likes and dislikes about the food (make it fun).

2. Go bowling with other couples. Sometimes incorporating other couples can add more closeness between each other when you're paired on the same team.

3. When going out, play dress-up. Set a theme for what you're wearing on your date with each other, but get dressed in separate rooms of the house. In this exercise, try to pick something that you know they like a lot (don't be afraid to spice it up a little).

4. Go on dates once a week, and go on weekend getaways once a month. It does not have to be far, but just get

out of your usual surroundings (maybe the city an hour or two away is all you can afford; if so, that's far enough, you will see).

5. Movie night at home is a nice option as well. If you have kids, watch a movie with them, and once they're off to bed, cuddle up with your spouse and enjoy a nice movie night together.

6. Cook together. Cooking together is another good way to find out more about your spouse's secret family recipes, and it will spark up new conversations without any effort (it's something about the smell of food that heats up a marriage).

7. Go on a romantic vacation once a year. Look for a place that has time for a romantic moment, somewhere not so busy that you can't have a peaceful moment with each other. (I don't recommend busy cities until you've had romantic trips for a while.)

8. Go on spontaneous trips whenever the time is right. Believe me, you will know when it is time.

9. Go shopping together. You have to keep up with the times and exemplify newness in this area. (Again, it does not have to be expensive. It could be just a new bottle of cologne [for him] or a new pair of shoes [for her]. Just keep it fresh every chance you get.)

10. Board games are good to have around the house as well. This type of activity will keep the competitive side of the relationship popping in your marriage. It

doesn't hurt to make it a little interesting as well (if you know what I mean; you're married, it's okay).

11. Talk to each other spiritually. Maybe it's about the sermon you heard at church this week, or read with each other, maybe even watch a spiritual television program every now and then and have a discussion about it afterward. What I'm saying is do *not* lose sight of the covenant that you both share in your marriage; it is the very core that holds your marriage together whether you know it or whether you acknowledge it or not. (Pray together and pray for each other.)

12. Last but certainly not least, *have fun again with each other*!

I challenge you both to implement these simple activities into your marriage; you will begin to see an incredible change in each other's attitude as you show a spirit of commitment in your relationship. This will jump-start a world of new adventures that you can reminisce on while eating breakfast or over a candlelit dinner. All I know is that if you take one step, God will take two, so give each other all you got, and it will produce something that I am hoping these words in this book has helped you find, and that is *a great marriage*.

Discussion: This topic continues the trend of bringing fun in your marriage. Turn on that creative mind and go for it. It's time to give your marriage that fun and excitement that it's been longing for, and so have you.

Make your own list of things you want to do individually then support each other in them as a whole. Don't make your list seem the more important of the two; they are to both be treated with the same excitement and enthusiasm. I want both of you to reap the benefits of all your hard work and create long-lasting memories together. It's something you both deserve!

Husband

_____
_____
_____
_____
_____
_____
_____
_____
_____
_____
_____
_____
_____
_____
_____
_____
_____
_____
_____
_____
_____
_____

Wife

Sex in Marriage

I decided to save this portion of your marriage-finding quest until the very end for a couple of reasons. I knew because it's a subject that, in order to be able to enjoy its full purpose, requires focus and freeness of the mind and body. But before I go any further, let's read what the Word of God says about this subject, and let's see the importance he puts on sex pertaining to married couples.

> The husband should fulfill his wife's sexual needs, and the wife should fulfill her husband's needs. The wife gives authority over her body to her husband, and the husband gives authority over his body to his wife. Do not deprive each other of sexual relations, unless you both agree to refrain from sexual intimacy for a limited time so you can give yourself more completely to prayer. (1 Corinthians 7:3–5, NLT)

Here's my take on that. It's easy to have great sex when your vision is not cloudy with all the things that has happened over time in your marriage. Having a clear vision of your wife/husband is vitally important to really have a great sexual experience as a couple.

When we read this text, it's really saying you have to be able to have sex even when you don't feel like it and if you are tired, if your husband/wife wants to have relations, then you are obligated to satisfy that need. Some of you, if you have not taken the focus off what your spouse did in the past or what they may have said, then you may need to revisit the first portion of this book to make sure you're ready to submit in this crucial ingredient in your marriage.

I don't know if you notice the sacrifice that God put on us in this area of our marriage. He is instructing us to give up our selfish nature to satisfy our partner in an area he knows if ignored could have a detrimental effect on the success of your marriage. So I encourage you to not deprive your spouse in this area because playing games like "holding out" on your husband/wife to the gain control over them could cost you your marriage. This intimate sacrifice should be an enjoyable experience for both, as we read in this text. We have to strive to "fulfill" the needs of our partner, which means to me that we need to know what "fulfills" them in this area. And how do we find out? We ask. This may be an awkward question to ask at first, but hopefully by reading this book, you have tuned the station to a new wave of communication.

We as married couples have to stop being afraid to enjoy this part of our marriage as if something is wrong with sex because the world does not mind painting a picture of its version of sex. I believe we can have that same enthusiasm that they have, but the difference is we have acquired knowledge and wisdom through the Holy Spirit that is more tasteful and more respectful to the person we are married to without the sin. Proverb 19:2 (NLT) says, "Enthusiasm without knowledge is no good; haste makes mistakes."

I want to encourage you to ask the questions you need to ask to get the knowledge and wisdom you need to succeed in this vital part of your marriage. Don't take it lightly; the enemy is waiting for the opportunity to sneak in with secret desires like pornography, lustful eyes, social media, and TV. We have to be strong and most of all "fulfilled" in this area without fail because this is where most of us appear to have secret desires and a selfish nature. So we must not neglect to die to ourselves daily in order to obtain victory in this battle.

Your Go to Play

"Go to play" is sports terminology that means whenever a team is in a situation where they're not playing well or if they're in need of a score, they run the play that is sure to get them a big play or a sure score. When the crowd noise is deafening and players don't have their head in the game, the coach simply goes *back to the basics*; he runs a play that calms the whole team down. This is what I believe we have to do in marriage; when things get offtrack, we simply need to go back to the basics—*love and respect*. This play will not fail. Why? Because God called the play, that's why. It will get your marriage back in the game and calm both players down again. Don't let the noise around you get you off your game, talk to one another daily, develop a deep friendship, and keep the *view* clear and focus on the prize, which is a great marriage.

Keeping your view of each other is so important to your marriage, so be careful not to pile up imaginary rocks in front of yourself; just because you can't see them doesn't mean that they don't exist. It could be that you're making accusations or embarrassing them in front of friends, bringing up the past issues that you claim you have forgiven them for just to prove a point or when in an argument. The rocks pile up fast, so when you see a rock fall, kick it away as quick as possible before it becomes the beginning of something you've worked so hard to fix. What happens when they are not kicked away (by way of acknowledgement or conversation) every time your wife/husband looks at you, they won't see you, they will see everything you have said and done that was not right or hurt them. You must do it as a team, but if you feel something inside, remember you have to communicate your feelings, you can't just expect them to always know when they have put their foot in their mouth, but do it all in love and respect. It's okay to do a daily check, like to see if there is anything you may have said or done that could be a potential rock at your feet.

Learn to say "I'm sorry" or "I didn't mean that"; it's part of running the play that God called you to run in your marriage. You have to give up a part of yourself to get what you need from the person you love; it's called a *sacrifice*. Give, and it shall be given; it works in life and in every situation.

I believe everything happens for a reason; you just have to stay around long enough to see what that reason is. It could be the result of a bad decision you may have made somewhere in the past, or it could simply be that it happened to mature you in a certain area that needs correction and you can't see. It's time to stop allowing divorce to be the only option or the cure to our marital problem. Deal with your issues in the most loving and respectful way that you both can. We are not—and we will never be—perfect nor is the person you married, we are all a work in progress. I love these scriptures in the Bible.

> People who except discipline are on the pathway to life, but those who ignore correction will go astray. (Proverbs 10:17)

> To learn, you must love discipline; it is stupid to hate correction. (Proverbs 12:1)

As you both continue in your marriage and face things of the unexpected world, look at them differently than you have before. Remember all of the corrections you have made and everything you've learned, and laugh, laugh, laugh at the enemy's same old attacks. If it's one thing I know, and this is my own quote, "If you don't give him *something* new, he want have *nothing* new."

> So humble yourselves before God. Resist the devil, and he will flee from you. (James 4:7)

My Testimony of God Clearing What I Call Cloudy Vision

As I was writing this book, the Lord began to deal with me on how my life experiences can benefit others because, as you may know, everything you go through in life is not just for you. I believe your testimony is not only to glorify God but is also a testament to say if he can do it for them, then he can do it for me as well. Amen to that. I talked a good portion on the aspects of keeping your vision clear, and it's important as it relates to your marital relationship. I was a victim, and now I'm a victor in this area of my marriage, I call it a case of "cloudy vision."

My testimony goes like this. My wife and I have had our share of ups and downs as well in our marriage at one point, that's the main reason I felt compelled to write this book in the first place. Because you can't tell someone else how to come out of something you haven't gone through yourself, anyway. I was unhappy, and so was she. I was fighting with my ex-wife about what's best for our kids that we had together, and I didn't agree with her choices at all. Also, the fact that my kids were living in another state didn't make things any better. At the time I didn't feel like my wife supported me enough in this already difficult time in my life, but boy, was I blinded by cloudy vision. I lost sight of my marriage in the worst way; more importantly, I lost sight of who my wife was in the midst of all the clouds. I was downright blinded by the enemy, and my marriage was headed for divorce.

So eventually things got worse, and I decided to do the worst thing you can do when having problems—*leave*. Whatever you do, don't *leave*. I can say this because I not only left my wife, but I left my best friend as well, but God is still God, and he knew I was not thinking straight and didn't know what in the world I was doing to my life and to the wife I believe he had for me. In my selfish and thoughtless decision to pursue what I believe was the best thing for my kids, I didn't realize my decision not only affected my wife but everybody around me.

I believed I had to do it on my own. I didn't trust God enough to do it. I had to show everybody I was right, and this is what I have to do. After leaving for a week and a half, my once cloudy vision that I had created for my wife was finally clear enough for me that this was not a good idea at all. Fortunately for me, my wife's vision for me was not clouded by my foolish decision to leave. What' so astonishing to me is how quickly we lose sight of our spouse in the midst of the clouds that sometimes hover over life and relationships. What you don't realize at the time is that clouds come and go with the wind, and in the end, the sun always follow closely behind.

But for me it got worse. I was diagnosed with colon cancer shortly after we decided to give our marriage another shot. It was a scary time for the both of us, and I didn't know what the outcome of this situation was going to be. But when I think of all the encouragement and support my wife was giving me in spite of what I had done, it was remarkable. I don't know what I would have done without her in my life at that point and don't want to find out either.

So long story short, God healed me of colon cancer—a big *amen* to that. My wife and I, being friends before we were married and along with the help of God, we were able to bounce from this potential tragedy by unknowingly using these practices I wrote in this book. From that point to this point, we put God first over all the chatter around us, and day by day our vision we once had started to become clearer and clearer. As you well know, things don't just go away overnight, but clouds started to cover all of the wrong, and the sun started to shine on our marriage.

What I want you to get from my own experience is that things happen in life and especially in marriages. There are going to be trials and tribulations, but when we get married, we agree that we are going to hang in there through these times. So we need to keep our commitment to one another and stop divorcing because of cloudy vision. Ask God to help move clouds daily that try to darken the marriage you had so high hopes for in the beginning of your marriage. Put God first in every situation that you face and know that it's only a test.

CONTRACT

I have read and have come to an agreement with all the information that is written in this book and I will to the best of my ability apply all that I have learned to my marriage. I will not use this information for no other reason except to uplift or encourage my husband/wife in our marriage going forward.

By signing this document you are both agreeing that this is a covenant between husband and wife.

_____

Husband Signature

_____

Wife Signature

Standing on Hope

Love
Love bears all things,
Believes all things, Hopes all things.
—1 Corinthians 13:7 (NKJV)

Believe
All things are possible to him who believes.
—Mark 9:23 (NKJV)

Faith
Faith is the substance of things hoped for, the
evidence of things not seen.
—Hebrew 11:1 (NKJV)

When you have bad days (and you will), just keep
going, but don't let the bad times dictate what your
marriage is worth.

Every day is simply a chance to get better, not worse.